I0161303

Stories My Daddy Told Me

By
Evelyn Wagner

Illustrations by
Letha Mitchell

TEACH Services, Inc.
P U B L I S H I N G
www.TEACHServices.com

World rights reserved. This book or any portion thereof may not be copied or reproduced in any form or manner whatever, except as provided by law, without the written permission of the publisher, except by a reviewer who may quote brief passages in a review.

This book was written to provide truthful information in regard to the subject matter covered. The author assumes full responsibility for the accuracy of all facts and quotations as cited in this book. The opinions expressed in this book are the author's personal views and interpretation of the Bible, Spirit of Prophecy, and/or contemporary authors and do not necessarily reflect those of TEACH Services, Inc.

This book is sold with the understanding that the publisher is not engaged in giving spiritual, legal, medical, or other professional advice. If authoritative advice is needed, the reader should seek the counsel of a competent professional.

Copyright © 2009, Revised 2012 TEACH Services, Inc.
ISBN-13: 978-1-57258-567-6 (Paperback)
ISBN-13: 978-1-57258-841-7 (Epub)
ISBN-13: 978-1-57258-842-4 (Kindle/Mobi)

Library of Congress Control Number: 2008938797

Published by
TEACH Services, Inc.
P U B L I S H I N G
www.TEACHServices.com

Table of Contents

Values
Priorities
and a
God Who
Cares

*This book is dedicated to Otto Mitchell's
great-grandchildren:*

*Jeremy Blair
Megan Blair
Shelley Blair Lanier
Bonnie Mitchell
William Mitchell
Christopher Wagner
Eric Wagner*

Foreword

*By Pastor Frank McMurry for
Otto Mitchell's Memorial Service*

Otto Mitchell was born June 21, 1899 in Height O'Land, Minnesota, to Charley and Anna Mitchell. He was the youngest of four children, having two older sisters, Anna and Clara, and an older brother, Charley.

Otto remembered his dad telling two young men they would get the worst beating of their lives if they harmed the young Seventh-day Adventist preacher who was holding meetings in the schoolhouse. He also remembered that when he was three years old he saw his dad put all his tobacco in the old stove and burn it. His parents and an older sister were baptized into the Seventh-day Adventist Church about that time.

Otto grew up in a loving, close family, but he was the only child in the family who ever received a spanking—a spanking he never forgot. He never spanked his children, but made right living attractive by his own example.

Otto worked hard to support his family, but wasn't afraid to give of his time and act promptly when a neighbor was in need. In the days when physicians made house calls, he would quickly drive to town and bring the doctor. (There were no telephones in that part of the country yet.) When another neighbor was about to lose his farm, Otto persuaded the banker to give the man a little more time on his loan, saving the man's home and living.

When a new neighbor moved in, sick, out of wood, and with little money, Otto brought wood, chopped it up and then had to convince the neighbor's wife that he was not selling wood, just helping.

The family remembers a lifetime of acts of kindness to others—a life with God the center of all his decisions. He loved life and wanted and hoped to live until Jesus came.

Otto married Marjorie Kendall at Battle Ground, Washington, June 19, 1930. She was 19 and he was 30. They settled in Jefferson, Oregon, where their children Bob and Evelyn were born, and Otto raised hay and kept cows. There was no Christian school in the Jefferson area, so when Bob was eight, they moved to Falls City, Oregon, where they ran a chicken farm. After four years there, the damp climate was giving health problems to Otto and especially to Bob. The doctor told Otto if he wanted to keep his son, he must move to a dryer climate, so in 1943 they moved to Terrebonne, Oregon. This was the family home for thirty-four years until they retired and moved to Rogue River. In Terrebonne he raised potatoes, alfalfa and sweet corn.

Here in Rogue River, Otto always had a large garden which he enjoyed working. He hadn't had much time for gardening during his farming years. Otto was planning a little smaller garden for the coming summer, because he had decided that at age 97 a big garden was just too much for him to keep up.

With his ability to be an active laborer slowing down, Otto now had more time to retell the stories that were a record of his life. His daughter Evelyn had started writing them out for a possible book. She would transcribe his narratives; then Otto would correct them or fill in the parts that were needed to round out all the parts.

On March 1, 1997, Otto suffered a major stroke. He never spoke again, and died March 10, at the Providence Hospital in Medford, knowing that the next thing he will see is his Savior Jesus. What a story that will be!!!

Foreword (Part II)

Stories My Daddy Told Me is a simply told, true and powerful chronicle of life in America—from pioneer days to a recent past now scarcely remembered. Evelyn's "Daddy" was a man to be trusted, whether telling his little girl about his adventurous grandfather and father's fearless skill with gun or rifle in tense disputes or his own escapades including perilous escapes (God-deliverances) from robberies of all types.

Evelyn's recollections of her father and mother's quiet trust in God in moments of peril and blessing, exemplifies Christianity and practical common sense at its best. Once "into" the story, its reality pulls you into a world almost forgotten now—where honest and manual labor were rewarded with the respect of man and blessing of God. If you're like me, this book will grab you and bless you . . . and you won't want to put it down!

—Juanita Kretschmar

Preface

I have happy memories of my childhood. As we sat around the table for the evening meal, Daddy could turn most any event into an exciting story, sharing what had happened during the day. It may have been helping a neighbor whose cow was sick, one who got his tractor stuck, someone who needed wood, or maybe just a conversation with the new neighbor who had moved out to the country and did not know a thing about farming or where the boundary fences were on the new farm he had just gotten.

After the dishes were done, the cows milked, the chickens fed and shut up for the night and all the animals taken care of, we usually had time to sit around the fire and listen to stories. After evening worship, I brought my pictures to color or something to draw while my brother, Bob, would be tinkering on anything that needed fixing, as we listened to the stories our parents shared. Sometimes Mother read to us. Sometimes Daddy would tell us stories of when he was a small boy or what it was like during the long Minnesota winters.

I treasure Daddy's stories and now want to share a few of them with you.

—Evelyn Wagner

Chapter 1

America the Beautiful

We hold these truths to be self-evident, that all men are
created equal...that they are endowed by their Creator...
with certain unalienable rights, that among these are:
Life, Liberty and the pursuit of happiness.

The "shot heard round the world" fired at Lexington on April 19, 1775 began the war for American independence. The thirteen colonies had joined together in the American Revolution against the mother country. They adopted the Declaration of Independence in 1776 and became the United States.

Great Britain had undertaken a new colonial policy intended to tighten political control over the colonies and to make them pay a tax and return revenue to the mother country. The tax caused a great deal of anxiety among the New England merchants.

April 19, 1775, shots had been exchanged by colonials and British soldiers, men had been killed, and a revolution had begun. The Green Mountain Boys, together with a force under Benedict Arnold, took Fort Ticonderoga from the British. Boston was under British siege, and before that siege was climaxed by the costly British victory usually called the battle of Bunker Hill, the Congress had chosen George Washington as commander in chief of the Continental American Forces.

The British gave up Boston in March, 1776, but the prospects were still not good for the ill-trained, poorly armed volunteer soldiers of the Continental Army when the Congress declared the independence of the thirteen colonies.

Benjamin Franklin, John Adams, and others were striving to get help. The leaders in the new country were those prominent either in the counsel halls or on the fields of the Revolution. Some of the more radical Revolutionary leaders were disappointed in the turn toward conservatism after the Revolution was over, but liberty and democracy had been fixed in the highest ideals of the United States.

Not only was this the beginning of American history, it was also the beginning of the Mitchell family in America.

Chapter 2

Thanks for the Ride to America

While the war raged for American independence, my great-great-grandfather lived in Scotland serving as a soldier in the Scottish army. At that time, Great Britain began hiring Scottish soldiers to come to America to fight against the Colonists. My dad's great-grandfather was one of the many soldiers put on a mighty sailing ship and brought to America to help the British fight against the new country struggling for its independence.

This was an exciting adventure for the young soldier as he traveled the high seas to the new world. Some of the men were happy to come to America. Some of them hated the idea, but there was one thing they agreed on. They did not want to fight the citizens of this new country.

The soldiers carefully, secretly, and very courageously decided on a plan as the sailing vessel sliced through the waves of the Atlantic Ocean. These brave Scottish soldiers agreed on a brash unthinkable escapade. What would happen? No one knew.

The ship continued to plow through the storms in its way and conquered the twenty-foot waves it faced at times. When it finally reached American soil, a shipload of well-trained Scottish soldiers joined the army under George Washington and fought along with the American soldiers against the British.

When the war was over, Great-Great-Grandfather became a loyal citizen here—in the land of the free and the home of the brave. He was always thankful for the thrilling way for him to have gotten a free ride to America and to become a part of this new and wonderful country.

Chapter 3

Heading West

Grandpa Mitchell was born in New York in 1855. His dad sailed around the world placing the American Ambassadors in other countries. He also made five trips around the Cape Horn of South America, and the crew sailed to the Oregon and Washington coasts and caught whales from a whaling vessel. They made oil from the fat of the whale and also took the whalebone back around the Cape Horn of South America to the East Coast to sell. This was a thriving business at that time in the history of America.

After Grandpa's father died and his mother remarried, home became a place where he did not want to be. He had an aunt in California who had gotten rich in the gold rush. She wanted to adopt Grandpa. She said she had put $25,000 in the bank for him, and he could have it when he became twenty-one years old. What an opportunity for a young man!

Tempted by the thought of all that wealth, he left home and headed for California.

Grandpa traveled as far as Illinois where two of his uncles had formed a wagon making company which they called The Mitchell Company. The uncles tried to get Grandpa to become a part of the company, but he did not want to become a part of The Mitchell Company. He had $25,000 on his mind, and he planned to go to California and get it.

Grandpa joined the next wagon train heading west. The early spring weather made the roads wet and sloppy, and because the horses were already having a hard time pulling the heavily loaded wagons, the men and boys walked behind. This helped to keep the wagonload as light as possible, but Grandpa's feet got wet and cold. He became deathly sick with pneumonia. With no way to take care of Grandpa on the wagon train, he was taken to a little cabin beside the road and left to die.

An old man and lady lived in the little cabin. The man had been a soldier in the North and South War and had one leg shot off. This was long before modern medicine, but people did their best, usually caring for the sick at home. The old lady knew about hydrotherapy treatments—an age-old natural cure. The way it works is simple. By increasing circulation in the body, hydrotherapy increases circulation of white blood cells, which stimulate the immune system. The drawing of blood to and through targeted areas of the body stimulates the immune system, detoxifies the body, heals injured tissues, re-energizes the body and more.

This dear old lady put her hydrotherapy knowledge to work, and used hot and cold fomentation treatments to save my grandpa's life. His shirt was removed and he lay on his back while the lady put a dry towel on his bare chest and stomach. Into a big pot of boiling water she dipped another towel and twisted it around till as much water as possible was squeezed out. She then placed it on top of the dry towel and put another dry towel on top. She kept Grandpa's chest as warm as possible with hot, damp towels for nearly fifteen minutes while trying not to burn him. Then she removed the towels and rubbed his chest with a damp ice-cold towel or whatever piece of cloth she had for a few seconds. This she repeated three times, and his chest became pink from the process. Next Grandpa was turned on his stomach and the whole procedure was repeated on his back.

By morning, Grandpa felt better. After resting a few days, he got up, but was dreadfully disappointed to find that he had no shoes. The old lady had put his shoes too near the fire to dry, and it cooked the leather. The shoes fell apart when Grandpa tried to put them on. The poor old lady felt horrible about her mistake, but nothing could be done about it. Grandpa stayed with the couple and helped the old man cut timber. In this way he made enough money to get another pair of shoes.

When the next wagon train came along, Grandpa joined it. This wagon train was on its way to North Dakota and was carrying a sawmill which had been taken apart to move, but when it arrived at its destination, no one knew how to put it together. Grandpa could do about anything, so he stayed around a few weeks and helped assemble the portable sawmill. Then he worked on the engine and got it running. Everything was ready to begin sawing down the trees and making them into lumber when unthinkable and dreaded events began to happen.

Chapter 4

Indians!!

Horses and cattle were an important part of the lives of the people who had traveled to North Dakota. There were no fences, and someone herded the stock while others worked at the sawmill or around their places getting ready to make lumber and build their new houses and sheds for the animals.

One terrifying morning Indians rode in on horseback. It didn't take them long to round up most of the horses and drive them away toward the hills. Grandpa didn't know anything about Indians, but when he heard the Indians had come, he wanted to see what they looked like. He ran outside and up a little hill. One of the Indians saw Grandpa, turned his horse around, and came riding back. Grandpa ran for his life for a buffalo wallow.

Buffalo wallows are holes in the ground that the buffalo made by rolling around to get the flies off their backs. Grandpa ducked down in a buffalo wallow grabbing a rock in each hand. When the Indian rode up with his gun, Grandpa threw a rock and hit the horse. The horse started bucking, and the Indian started shooting. Grandpa kept hitting the horse with rocks to keep the horse frightened and jumping around and kept the Indian from shooting straight.

Someone from the mill heard the shooting and rushed out with a gun and shot the Indian. When the Indian rolled off his horse, Grandpa ran over and grabbed the Indian's gun and shell belt and ran back to the hole. By this time there were about a dozen Indians coming after my grandpa. When they saw him get the gun, they stopped and shot at him a few times, but did not hit him, then turned around and rode off catching up with the others who had the stolen horses.

What were they to do? They couldn't run a sawmill without horses to haul in the logs. It was frightening, but a few brave men said that they would go and get those horses back. Grandpa and five other men got guns and plenty of ammunition. They followed the Indians for three days. An older man, whom everyone called California Joe, was the leader. The young men looked to him for guidance. As the fellows hurried out of the timber and into more of the prairie country, California Joe said, "We don't dare go down through this draw because the Indians may be waiting for us and would kill every one of us. We had better go up on that hill and look down and see if the Indians have gotten there yet."

When the men reached the top of the hill they saw the Indians hiding in the gully waiting for them. Grandpa said there were thousands of Indians out across the prairie. Never before had he seen so many people gathered together. He knew they were ready for war.

What was happening? What were the Indians planning? With their blood turning to ice, the horses didn't seem as important to Grandpa and his companions as they rushed back to the woods and hid. Feeling their lives were at stake, they stayed hidden for several days. Would the Indians come back and kill or capture them?

Chapter 5

Danger

Letha Mitchell

The Indians Grandpa and the other man had seen were gathering horses and braves to meet General Custer and his men for battle. History tells us there were many thousands of Indians gathered ready for war. This battle is now known as "Custer's Last Stand" and "The Battle of the Little Bighorn."

Custer's men expected the Indians to fight them with bows and arrows, but the Indians had guns that were very dangerous at short range. The Indian ponies could outrun the soldier's horses, so General Custer had asked for guns that could shoot long distances. Most of the guns General Custer and his men had could be shot only once and then needed to be loaded again. The guns the Indians carried held thirteen shells which could be pumped out one right after the other. Custer's troops were no match for these well-armed Indians, and in 1876 they were completely annihilated.

After Custer's Massacre, the government sent out General Miles. General Miles came to where Miles City, Montana, stands today. Grandpa went up the river on a paddle wheel steamboat to help build a fort there. He and the men went on shore and set up camp. The captain of the steamboat, frightened and cruel, gathered the few soldiers he had with him, and without telling Grandpa or his companions, fled during the night taking the soldiers down the river to a safer place. He left my grandpa and the other men who had come to help build the fort stranded on the river bank alone without any protection. The men did not dare to make any noise or even build a fire. They feared for their lives and had to stay hidden. What would happen if the Indians knew they were there? Hordes of mosquitoes had a feast. The men had no protection from them—not even smoke from a fire.

About a week later, a paddle wheel steamboat loaded with soldiers came up the river. It, along with the soldiers, stayed until Grandpa and the other men built Fort Keogh. After the fort had been built, the men felt much safer. That fort became home, and Grandpa lived there for several years before deciding he wanted to travel elsewhere.

When the time came for him to leave Fort Keogh, he made himself a boat, put the boat in the river, loaded in all of his possessions, climbed in, and headed out to an unknown adventure.

Chapter 6

"Take 'Em Out, Mac"

letha mitchell

Alone in his homemade boat, Grandpa followed the Missouri River all the way to Bismarck, North Dakota. After arriving somewhere near Bismarck, he knew this would be a good place to live, so he set up residence.

Grandpa became acquainted with a couple of other men, and they started raising cattle together. When the other two men told my grandpa they were not going to cut grass to make hay for the winter, he parted company with them. He took one third of the cattle as his piece of the partnership and worked all summer putting up hay for the winter. That winter turned very cold, but he had hay for his cattle. The other two men lost all of their cattle, for the cattle had no food to eat. Grandpa lost only one cow that had fallen over a snow bank. He had not found it in time to save its life.

One morning Grandpa looked out the window of his small cabin and noticed a bunch of horses eating at his haystack. *Well! I can't have those horses eating all of my hay* he told himself. He called Mac, his dog, and told him to take the horses out of there. The horses all wheeled and ran across the prairie. The next morning Grandpa saw three men on horseback driving the horses back to his haystack. He took Mac and his rifle and rode out to meet the men. One of the men said, "If you sic your dog on our horses we will shoot him." Grandpa did not say a word. He just pulled the hammer back on his rifle and told Mac to "take 'em out." The horses wheeled around and ran. The three men followed their horses galloping across the prairie. He never saw those horses or men again.

Grandpa loved animals and made pretty good money raising big work horses. He stayed at this place for several years and felt he was having a good life. He never anticipated and never could have imagined the challenges and changes in the future that God had waiting for him.

Chapter 7

New Friends, the Indians

Indian tribes were willing to live with the newcomers until relations were strained as more and more people took away their land and resources. The government encouraged its citizens to move to Oregon Territory. This took land away from the Indians. Sometimes they were defensive and aggressive. The government created Indian Reservations which were large tracts of land specifically for the Indians to dwell on. The transition to reservation life was not easy, but the Indians had little choice.

Grandpa lived close enough to the Indian Reservation to become acquainted and make friends with them. Because the Indians trusted Grandpa, they taught him many skills.

He said that if an Indian trusted you, he would become your most loyal friend. Indians are a proud, independent people, and Grandpa felt they were treated very unfairly. Because of the fear of more massacres, the settlers did not trust the Indians. Their fear was real because some of the Indians were out to kill.

One day Grandpa came home in time to see two Indians running out of his house with his blankets. He shouted for them to drop the blankets, but they kept running. He shot a bullet about two feet away from them, and they dropped the blankets and kept going.

A few days later, an Indian Grandpa didn't know was knocking at his door. Grandpa opened the door with a gun in each hand. "I have come to tell you," the Indian said. "There are two men who have vowed to kill you. You must be careful." Grandpa felt grateful for an Indian who risked his life to save a white man.

He took the Indian outside and said, "Do you see that rock over there? It is about the size of a man's head." Then he took his gun, and even though the rock was a long ways from where he and the other man were standing, he fired and hit it dead center. "Now," he said, "tell those men if I ever see either one of their faces, I will shoot."

Grandpa was not a Christian at the time. He did not know the Lord. These were the days of the Wild West, and it took courage to survive. However, my dad did not believe Grandpa ever killed anyone. Grandpa realized years later that even though he did not know there was a God, it was God who kept him alive and kept him from harming another.

Later, there was an uprising. The Indians wanted to be free, and they planned to do whatever it took to make this happen. The Cavalry again captured the Indians and brought them back to the reservation. When one of the men who had tried to steal Grandpa's blankets came past his house in the wagon, he covered his head with a blanket so Grandpa could not see his face.

My grandpa became well acquainted with, and a good friend of the great Chief Sitting Bull. Chief Sitting Bull was the chief of the Sioux Tribe and had lead thousands of warriors in days gone by. It was he and his warriors who Grandpa had seen that fateful day many years before as he looked out on the valley and saw thousands and thousands of Indians gathering for the battle of the Little Bighorn.

Now Chief Sitting Bull was an old man. He had been a great and fearless warrior who was respected and feared by many. By this time, he lived in a little cabin not far from where Grandpa lived, and he liked to visit Grandpa when he could.

One day Grandpa and Chief Sitting Bull were out looking at the horses. Chief Sitting Bull said, "Hey Charley, have you named that colt yet?" Chief Sitting Bull stood studying a fine-looking chestnut colt. Grandpa said, "No." Chief Sitting Bull said, "Call him Bull." From that day on, that beautiful horse was called "Bull."

Another Indian left a pair of snowshoes with Grandpa. "Keep these for me until I come back for them." he told Grandpa. Years later when they all moved to Oregon, Grandpa insisted on bringing the snowshoes. "I told that old Indian I would keep the snowshoes until he came back for them, and that is exactly what I plan to do," Grandpa said. *

Grandpa was a young bachelor. Life was good, but he was missing something. He felt a bit lonely at times and knew the time had come for him to settle down and find someone with whom he could share his life, love, and whatever other adventures awaited him.

---

* Those snowshoes now hang on the wall in his great grandson William Mitchell's home in Klamath Falls, Oregon.

Chapter 8

Grandpa Meets the Girl of His Dreams

Grandmother's parents, Mr. and Mrs. Komm, came from Germany and settled in the Midwest. Later, they moved to a little town west of Bismarck called New Salem. A man by the name of Marcus Demure lived by New Salem. He owned the largest cattle ranch in the country. Mr. Demure hired Anna Komm to help in the cook shanty cooking for the cowboys.

That is where Grandpa met and became acquainted with Anna. He fell in love with the quiet, young lady, and they were married in about 1890.

Things did not go as they had planned. That summer a drought hit. The drought made survival almost impossible. Grandpa had been hearing about Minnesota, the land with lots of grass, hay, and water. He and Grandmother decided to move there. Grandmother's parents, four brothers and a younger sister wanted to go with them. They made themselves wagons, sold most of their cattle and horses, loaded up all of their worldly possessions, and started out for Minnesota.

Traveling slowly, they headed east towards Fargo, North Dakota. Grandmother had a big iron kettle that had come all the way from Europe. It rode under the wagon and was used to cook the evening meal over the fire. About one half mile before reaching the end of the journey the kettle hit a rock and broke. It was a big loss to everyone, but especially to Grandmother.

Homesteads were taken out about seventy miles beyond Fargo in the beautiful state of Minnesota. The homesteads were located on the north end of Height O'Land Lake and the south end of Rice Lake. The lakes were close together and the Ottertail River ran through their places.

Grandpa built a house by the river on a pleasant spot of land. He brought in eight-foot-long logs made from trees a foot in diamter, sawed these logs down the middle, and set them up vertical on a rock foundation. After white washing the house, it looked almost like a frame house (see picture on page 104). This is where my daddy, his brother, and two sisters were raised.

The Ottertail River emptied into Height O'Land Lake—a picturesque lake five miles across. Grandpa made a dam on the river, and it is still called Mitchell Dam. My daddy was three years old at the time and remembered watching him build that dam. The logs came twenty miles down the river and then went into the lake. After they were transported across the lake, the logs went twenty more miles down the river to a sawmill. It took several dozen men working with the logs to boom them together and take them across the lake with a paddle wheel steam boat. The boat was run by my daddy's uncle, Otto Comm, and Daddy felt like a pretty big man when he could go across the lake with all of those logs.

Even though Daddy was very young, he forever remembered the thrilling changes that were happening in their home and family. These were changes that Daddy was grateful for through the years as life began to take on new meaning.

Chapter 9

Learning New and Exciting Things

One day when Grandpa wasn't too busy, the family decided to visit some neighbors who lived across the lake. As Grandpa and his family were getting into the boat to go see the neighbors, they saw a boat coming up the river. They waited. Here came the family that Grandpa was planning to see, and with them, George Budd, a Seventh-day Adventist minister. They asked, "May we have meetings in your house?"

Grandpa, the foreman of the thirty or forty men working with the logs, said, "If you can help keep these men from getting drunk, you are welcome to have meetings in our home. They get paid and need their money for new clothes and new shoes, but they spend their money on drink and come back to work in rags."

Meetings were held in Grandpa's home until the crowd got too big, and Pastor Budd moved the meetings down the road a few miles to a vacant schoolhouse. This old schoolhouse made an excellent place to meet. More people were able to attend and enjoy listening to what Pastor Budd had to say.

When Grandpa and his family got to the meeting one evening, a crowd of people were standing around outside. The door to the schoolhouse was locked so no one could get in. A couple of young fellows were swaggering back and forth saying, "You folks might as well go home. There won't be any meeting tonight. We are going to go meet that preacher and give him a beating. We are going to tell him to get out of here and never come back, so all of you might as well go home right now!"

Pastor Budd walked along a trail that went around the lake to get to the meetings. Grandpa listened to what the two fellows were telling the people as he finished tying up the horses.

"Wait a minute!" he called. "Come back here!" Then he walked over to them and said, "If you ever lay hands on this preacher, I'll give both of you the beating of your lives."

They knew Grandpa could do it, so they didn't carry out their threat. The minister arrived, and everyone went to the meeting that night. There were several more meetings before someone on the school board said, "We will stop those meetings. We'll just nail boards across the door of the schoolhouse." That brought the meetings to a close.

A few weeks later, someone decided it would be fun to

have a dance, so the boards were pulled off the door of the schoolhouse, and it was opened for the dance. Horses and buggies came from all directions, and the schoolhouse filled quickly. It started raining right in the middle of the dance; the rain came down in sheets. The wind blew hard, screaming and howling. In its fury, it reached down, pulled the roof of the schoolhouse off, and carried it about one hundred feet away before dropping it to the ground. That schoolhouse was never used again.

Grandpa, Grandma, and Daddy's oldest sister, Anna, were baptized into the Seventh-day Adventist Church after hearing the wonderful, new message from the Bible. Daddy remembered Grandpa taking the lid off the old cook stove in the kitchen one evening and putting his pipe and all of his tobacco into the roaring fire. He had had his last smoke. All his kids felt they had the best Dad in the whole world.

Chapter 10

That First Little Bite

My daddy was just a little guy, but he remembered walking with his dad one evening going to the neighbors. They walked across a field in knee-deep snow. Daddy tried to step in his dad's tracks, but they were too far apart. Before they left for home, the neighbor, who had received a large box of apples from relatives in Oregon, handed each of them a big Red Delicious Apple. It was too cold to raise fruit where Daddy lived in Minnesota. They did not have fresh fruit to eat until the apples from Yakima, Washington, were shipped into the area.

That apple looked absolutely wonderful to Daddy. Grandpa put his in his pocket, so Daddy put his apple in his pocket too. In their family, whenever anyone got something special, they always shared it with the rest of the family. Daddy was the youngest and had two older sisters and a big brother.

Going across the snow-covered field, Daddy decided just to smell the apple. It smelled so good he wanted to take a little bite and figured that when his dad divided the apple, Daddy's piece could be where the little bite was taken. That bite was so good, Daddy could not seem to help but take another bite. The next bite was a little bigger. By the time they got home, he had eaten the entire tasty apple.

Daddy felt dreadful. *Now what was he going to do?* He thought hard and decided he would go right into the house and straight to bed before anyone heard about the apples.

Grandpa laid his apple on the table and said to Daddy, "Where is your apple?"

"I ate it all coming home," he answered. *Oh, dear. Why had he done it?* He just wanted to disappear and not face his big brother and sisters.

His brother and sisters said, "The pig. To think he ate the whole apple! Don't give him any of this one."

Grandpa said, "Mother, cut that apple into six pieces." Then turning toward Daddy who was hurrying in the direction of the ladder to go to the loft and the seclusion of his small bed, Grandpa said, "Otto, come back here and get your apple."

Daddy knew when Grandpa spoke, nobody argued, so he slowly ate his piece of apple. It tasted like a piece of bark, and he never forgot the lesson.

Chapter 11

The Birthday Candy

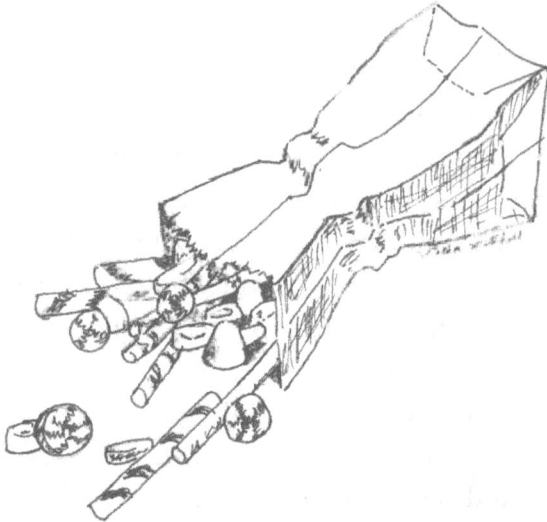

A boy in Daddy's class at school got a big bag of candy because it was his birthday, and his dad told him to go treat the boys at school. When my daddy was a boy, the girls played on one side of the school yard and the boys played on the other during recess. The boy came walking down the sidewalk out to the playground where the boys were. He had a pleased expression on his face whistling all the way. One of the boys said, "Look at him. He sure must be happy."

He started passing candy around to all of the boys and kept passing it around until the five minute bell rang. When the bell rang and all the boys started to go into the schoolhouse, he came to Daddy and pulled his coat pocket open. Then he poured in half of the rest of that big bag of candy.

Some of the other boys were surprised and asked, "Why

don't you give us some more, too?"

"I gave you all candy," he shrugged, "and Otto is the only one who said 'thank you.'"

The songs of the birds filled the air with music that day after school, and Daddy had enough candy to treat all the kids on the bus going home.

Chapter 12

Old Joe

Old Joe was a special person. He could not hear or talk, but Old Joe was Daddy's friend. He smiled at the kids, and talked to them making gestures with his hands. They did not know what he said, but they knew he liked them, and the kids liked him. There was one thing that everyone knew Old Joe liked to do. He liked to go out on the lake and fish from his little fishing boat. He was one good fisherman!

July 4, Independence Day, was a day Daddy and his siblings looked forward to all year. Grandpa had explained to them that on this day—the birthday of the wonderful, free country in which they lived—the United States had earned its freedom from the rule of Great Britain.

On July 4, the horses did not need to work in the fields. They did not need to cultivate the long rows of potatoes or corn, or cut and rake the big fields of sweet smelling hay. On July 4, they were hitched to the wagon, and Daddy and his family all climbed in and rode down the dusty road to the lake. Here they met the whole community who had come to celebrate the 4th of July.

Daddy said, "Our independence was something we could all celebrate together. We were proud of our country. We were proud of our community. We kids were proud of Dad. He believed in celebrating Independence Day together."

The day they looked forward to all year had finally arrived. There would be ice cream from the ice cream maker when the men finished turning the crank. Ice cream was a treat. With no refrigerators or freezers, they cut large chunks of ice from the lake and brought them to the fruit cellar during the long Minnesota winter. These big chunks of ice were part of the fruit cellar's walls. They were buried in sawdust to keep the ice from melting. This made a good, cool place to keep the potatoes, carrots, beets, and squash during the hot summer days that were sure to follow. Jars of food were canned all during the summer as the garden produced more than could be eaten by the family. These, too, were stored in the cool fruit cellar.

When it was time for the 4th of July celebration, ice was gathered from its precious hiding place and taken along to the picnic with thick cream and sugar to make home-made ice cream. The ice was placed around the container holding the cream, sugar, vanilla or other flavorings. Someone poured salt onto the ice to make it act faster, and then the work to make the delicious once-a-year treat began.

Truly this turned into a never to be forgotten day. The big boys were standing around in groups waiting for the food and taking turns cranking the handle of the ice cream maker. They looked busy, but all the time they were trying to make conversation with some of the girls who were helping at the tables.

Some of the men had driven iron stakes into the ground and were seeing who could throw a horseshoe the thirty feet away to make a ringer. Others were sitting around under the big oak trees visiting. Several men brought big, juicy watermelons from their watermelon patches and already put them into the cool water at the edge of the lake for an afternoon treat.

The smaller boys were down by the lake trying to see who could skip stones the farthest. Looking across the lake they saw Old Joe fishing, but who were those two people swimming around his boat? How could he catch fish with them stirring up the water? He tried to motion them to go swim somewhere else, but they thought it was more amusing teasing Old Joe and getting him angry with them.

"Let's have some fun," one of the young men shouted to the other. "Let's tip him out of the boat."

Old Joe could not hear what they said, but he was not about to be tipped out of the boat if he could help it. When one of the guys swam up and grabbed on to the little dinghy, Old Joe's oar came down on the hand so fast and hard that blood stained the water. The young man hastily swam to shore where he quickly got dressed. His companion did the same, and then they walked back and forth watching Old Joe.

"Wait until he gets here, and we'll give him a beating he will never forget," one of the men said to the other.

Even though Daddy was skipping stones out on the lake, he heard every word they said. Quickly he slipped away from the rest of his friends. He knew he was too little to do anything about it, but he had a big brother, and he ran to find him as fast as he could.

As soon as Daddy told his brother, Charley, what two men he had never seen before were planning to do to Old Joe, Charley and a group of his friends ran down to the lake. Daddy had to really run to keep up. Charley was the bravest person Daddy had ever known. At least he thought so.

Charley walked up to those two men and said, "If you beat up Old Joe, we will give you the worst thumping you ever want to see." Then he added, "And if anything ever happens to Old Joe, I will look you two up, and hold you personally responsible for it. Now get into your buggy, and get out of here. We don't want to ever see you again."

It did not take long for those two strangers to hitch the horse to the buggy; all they left behind was a cloud of dust. Daddy was tremendously proud of his big brother and felt he was the luckiest guy around. Old Joe never knew he had an army of kids looking out for him.

Chapter 13

The Unforgettable 4th of July

"Let's not join the crowd over on Little Floyd Lake to-day," the neighbor said. "Let's get a few families together and go over to Big Floyd Lake."

Little Floyd Lake had a big campground with lots of pic-nic tables. That is where Daddy and his family usually went on the 4th of July to celebrate Independence Day.

When Daddy's mother told them what the neighbor said, they all agreed that it would be fun to go to Big Floyd Lake for a change. An interesting building had been built at the lake with poles for the framework. Someone cutting wood had peeled the bark off and then had laid the bark out to dry with a weight placed on top of the bark to straighten it out. The bark was about sixteen inches wide after it became flat. This material was used to cover the outside of the poles, and the building was called The Bark Shanty although it was quite large and used as a lodge.

A club of about twenty girls from North Dakota had come to camp at The Bark Shanty for a vacation, but this day they had gone home to celebrate Independence Day with their families.

That morning Daddy's mother and his sisters packed a big lunch. There was home-made bread made from the wheat they had grown and then taken to the mill to be ground into flour. The sweet, fresh butter to be eaten with the bread had been made the day before.

After milking the cows, the milk was poured into pans to sit overnight. During the night, the cream rose to the top of the milk. Then they removed the cream with a big spoon and put it into a churn. Daddy or one of his siblings would make the churn's handle go around and around to keep the cream moving for nearly an hour. Little specks of butter began to form and gradually turned into the half pound of butter they usually made each time. The liquid left in the churn was the buttermilk used to make the fluffy pancakes they all enjoyed for breakfast.

Grandmother took a jar of pickles made from the cucumbers that had grown in the garden the summer before. The three-layer cake, made from fresh eggs from the chicken house and sweet thick cream, was carefully placed in the large lunch basket. With a big crock of baked beans hot from the oven, the lunch was ready to go.

The boys and Grandpa had milked the cows and put them out to pasture. The chickens, ducks, and turkeys had been fed. Their dog, Jack, had eaten a good breakfast, and the three barn cats had drunk their dish of milk, to add to the many mice they caught behind the sacks of feed stored in the barn.

No one seemed concerned about the weeds that had poked their little heads through the rich moist soil in the garden, or the vegetables that needed to be harvested. This was a day they did not need to carry water from the well to put on the old kitchen stove in a large container used to heat water so Grandmother and her two daughters could wash the laundry in the big wash tub. This was the 4th of July, and they were celebrating together.

Before dinner, Daddy and two of his friends decided to get into a boat and go fishing. One of the fellows, they called Red, had come on his bicycle to have dinner with them. Red went exploring. He went to The Bark Shanty and found a red and white girl's swimsuit. Slipping into the swimsuit, he came down to the lake and started swimming around being the clown of the day.

"Come on in. The water is fine," he would squeak trying to make his voice sound like a girl's and still loud enough so everyone could hear.

After he got tired of that, Red decided to swim out to his friends in the boat. Daddy watched him coming. The others in the boat were looking another direction. Daddy saw Red's head drop, and then he disappeared.

"Pull the anchor!" Daddy shouted to the others. "Head towards the shore!"

He tried to keep his eyes on the spot where Red had gone under. The lake was about ten feet deep there. They stopped at the place where Daddy had last seen Red, and saw bubbles coming up. Glenn would stay in the boat while Ellsworth and Daddy planned to dive into the water and go down to find Red.

"Put down the anchor!" Daddy yelled. He could see the red and white swimming suit coming up. They reached out, grabbed the swimming suit, and pulled Red into the boat.

He was limp as a rag. Ellsworth and Daddy laid Red on his stomach across the boat seat. They pushed on his sides, let up and pushed again. They kept pushing the water out of his lungs while Glenn rowed toward shore.

When they pulled Red out of the boat, he sat up and started coughing. Water flew out of his lungs. He sat there awhile coughing and spitting out the water. After quite awhile Red seemed to feel better. He got on his bike and rode away, still wearing the girl's swimsuit.

Daddy always wondered if the girl ever got her swimming suit back.

Chapter 14

Time Moves On

The winters were hard. Daddy remembered going out and cutting twigs and brush so the sheep could eat the twigs to keep alive during the winter.

Many of the neighbors were getting sick. Some had gotten pneumonia. If one of the neighbors got pneumonia, they would usually send for Grandpa. He had learned a little trick from the Indians that he never forgot. They showed him how to cure pneumonia. He would take the fat from a skunk, cook it, and mix it with turpentine making it into a salve. When Grandpa heard of someone who wanted him to come because they had pneumonia, he would take a little container of his "cure" and head out into the weather no matter how cold it happened to be. If the horses could get down the road, he took the buggy or the sled. If the snowdrifts were too high, he would go on foot making his way through the storm by kerosene light if need be. After giving a treatment of rubbing the salve on the patient's bare chest and also on the back, he would leave enough of the "remedy" for several more treatments. Many people died that winter from pneumonia, but every person Grandpa treated survived.

Daddy's mother had not been well. The snow piled up to the tops of the fence posts, and Grandma ran out of medicine. Grandpa knew she would die if she did not get some medication. He got up one morning before daylight, took the old kerosene lantern, and headed for town. The wind had blown the snow off the lake so he crossed the lake on the ice and continued to walk the twenty miles to town. He bought the medicine and something to eat. Then he walked back home that night in about 40 degree below zero temperature.

That long walk through the snow was enough for Grandpa. He decided to sell the home place and move closer to town. "We are too far from help." He said. "Someone might die before we could get the aid we needed."

Grandpa bought eighty acres of land three miles north of Detroit Lakes. Here they built a large, two-story house where they lived for many years. On Sabbaths they went to church in different people's homes. Grandpa decided that the people needed to be able to worship in a church building, so he and two other men, who were carpenters, built a nice church building on a lot in town.

Grandma raised chickens and sold the eggs. Sometimes she traded eggs for something needed at the big General Store. Grandpa and his boys raised and sold horses. Uncle Charley and Daddy were young men by now, and Grandpa let them keep the horses they wanted. They had great horses—the best of any around.

Daddy's favorite horse was Little Beauty. She not only grew to be a handsome horse, but no horse around could outrun her. The banker's son tried to buy Little Beauty, but of course Uncle Charley and Daddy would not think of selling her. When another horse and buggy started to pass, if someone did not hold her back, a race was on. Little Beauty did not take to the idea of any horse passing her. She knew she was the best and liked to prove it. Daddy and his brother knew she was the best, too, and didn't mind letting people know they had the fastest horse on the road.

One day Grandpa said, "I don't know what is wrong with Little Beauty. I took her to town this morning and whenever another horse got close, she wanted to race. I had a hard time holding her." Uncle Charley and Daddy looked at each other. They figured Grandpa had a good idea what they had been doing.

It was a cold afternoon and the clouds continued dumping buckets of snow from the sky. Uncle Charley and Daddy were in town with Little Beauty, but evening was waiting for no one, and they decided they had better head home to do the chores. As they neared the train crossing, they saw a train coming, but it was quite far down the tracks. The flagman put up his flag and then looked at the train and motioned for them to cross the tracks.

When Little Beauty's foot hit the ice and snow covered crossing, she slipped and fell. The train started blowing its whistle and was bearing down on Daddy and Uncle Charley. It had no way to stop. Daddy sprang from the buggy and gave Little Beauty a kick that frightened her so badly she lunged forward getting herself on her feet. The wind held its breath. Little Beauty started out so fast that before you could even see her she was off those tracks and heading down the road. Daddy grabbed the back of the buggy as it flew past, and the train swished by on the track that was now just behind him.

Chapter 15

New Model T Ford

Letha Mitchell

The terrible Great War of 1914 to 1918 was being fought. The United States became a part of the fighting in 1917. Uncle Charley was called into the military and became a part of the first group of soldiers to have to go to another country to fight. Uncle Charley and Daddy had always done things together, and now he was far away. Daddy missed him terribly.

One evening Daddy decided there was no need to stay home and feel sorry for himself with a celebration in Detroit Lakes going on, so he got into their new 1916 Model T Ford and headed for the excitement.

On the way to town he stopped at his friend's house, but

he was not home. No one was home. Daddy stopped at another friend's home, and they were all gone, too. None of his friends were at home, so they must already be in town. Daddy drove on alone. It is not nearly as much fun when you are alone, but he felt sure he would be seeing them soon somewhere at the fair.

Daddy did not find it hard to find a place to park. Horses and buggies were everywhere. Some people had come on horseback. Others had come in wagons.

Daddy noticed two men, probably about twenty or maybe a little older. They were older and bigger than he was. They were all dressed up watching him as he took the key out of the car. All T Fords had the same key, but Daddy had made theirs different. He had put a piece of metal in the keyhole so no one could put a key in, and he had a tool to pull it out when he wanted to start the car. This way Daddy felt sure that no one could steal the car. When he glanced at those two big fellows watching him, he felt pleased he had fixed the keyhole in their car so no one could get another key in.

Daddy got out of the car and put the key in his pocket, then went to find his friends. He walked past some other cars to a place where candy was sold. His friends were not there. He passed other eating places, but could not find anyone he knew.

By this time, Daddy noticed that no matter where he went, the two young men were somewhere close by. They were following him! He suspected they were going to tackle him and steal the key to the car! *What was he going to do?* He looked for a policeman. Usually there were some around, but not tonight. He kept walking, looking for someone he knew. By now Daddy was sure these fellows wanted to get the car key away from him and take the car. The darkness was making its way in, ready to cover the fair grounds, but the lights at the entertainment booths continued to hold it back. As Daddy walked here and there, he kept trying to think of what he should do. *Where was someone he knew? Where was anyone he knew?*

This was not a situation that my daddy liked. It was getting late. Away from the lights of the entertainment everything flattened to blackness. He had seen nobody that he knew and felt very alone. All alone and two people were following him! He kept going from one display to another while acting very interested in what he saw, but Daddy was not paying any attention to the exciting things around him. He knew he was being watched, and it is not a good feeling to be all alone. *Was he really all alone?* No, Daddy was not alone. Hebrews 13 verse 5 came to his mind where it said Jesus would "never leave him nor forsake him."

Daddy began praying for the protection of his car and also protection for himself. He did not know what to do, but knew he had to do something soon. Daddy asked God what he should do. Then a plan began to formulate in his mind. He came to a place that was well lit, and a lot of farmers were standing around talking. They looked like pretty good people to Daddy. *If a fight starts with two big fellows against me,* he thought, *someone will come to my rescue.*

When Daddy got to the middle of the area, he quickly turned toward the fellows standing right behind him and spoke loudly, "Do you want to fight?"

This took them by surprise with everyone looking at them. They said, "No we don't want to fight," and walked behind the building.

As soon as they were out of sight, Daddy took off at a break-neck speed through the crowd straight for his car. He got it started as fast as he could, and that new Model T outdid itself full throttle ahead almost all the way home.

Through this experience Daddy realized that although he would not always be with his big brother, Charley, he was never alone. The Lord would always be watching out for him.

Chapter 16

The Best Dog a Fellow Ever Had

Letha Mitchell

Grandpa was getting old. The winters were so cold in Minnesota that he came west one winter and stayed with Daddy's oldest sister, Anna Jorgensen, and her husband, Chris. Anna had gotten married and moved to Jefferson, Oregon. Grandpa wrote home between Christmas and New Years saying he was wearing no coat and a short-sleeve shirt while picking apples off a tree. That same week the weather had turned so cold it had gotten 60 degrees below zero where Daddy lived in Minnesota. When Grandpa got back he said, "We are moving to Oregon."

Horses and buggies, wagons, and T Fords came down the driveway the day they had an auction sale. Most of their things were sold. They had already gotten a buyer for the farm they had called home for many years. The people who bought the place loved everything about it including Jack, the dog. Grandpa felt Jack had grown too old to move. The trip would be too hard on him. How would he survive the long way to Oregon on the train, anyway? Jack would be well taken care of right here at the home place. He would be happier staying where he had lived all of his life.

Leaving Jack behind about broke my daddy's heart. Daddy could go after the cows, walk in the woods, or go any other place knowing he was safe if Jack came with him. When an angry bull, with head down, came charging after Daddy, Jack grabbed the bull by the nose, and with one swift twist of his head, the bull found himself on his back before he hardly knew what was happening. Jack was usually very gentle with the cattle, but still the cattle soon learned to give him the respect he deserved.

When company came, and if the men or boys were standing around bragging about their dogs or whatever, it was fun for Daddy to turn the conversation towards Jack, who was generally close by his side. Daddy would say, "Jack, bring me a stick of oak wood from right over there," as he pointed towards the wood pile. My daddy named whatever kind of wood he wanted. Jack would run to the wood pile and start sniffing around.

"Look at that. He is actually looking for a stick of oak wood!" someone usually exclaimed as Jack became the center of attention. Finally Jack found what he wanted. He picked up the piece of wood, came over to Daddy, and laid it at his feet. The piece of wood he brought was always the right one—oak, birch, or whatever asked for.

"Let me have a look at that piece of wood. That's what it is. . . That's what it is. . . Wow!! What a dog! How can a dog tell the different kinds of wood?"

After they talked about how intelligent Jack was and

gave him lots of compliments, which he thoroughly enjoyed, Daddy told them what he had done. While the guys had been bragging about whatever, Daddy had slipped away and gone to the wood pile to rub his hands all over the piece of wood he wanted Jack to bring. Then he threw it up on the pile of wood, and Jack always found that piece of wood and brought it to Daddy.

Jack was the best dog a fellow could ever have, and now it was nearly time to tell him "goodbye." Daddy wondered if Jack would miss him as much as he would miss that dear old dog.

Chapter 17

Oregon, Oregon, Here We Come

The day came too soon when my daddy had to tell his friends and the home in which he had spent so many happy years "good bye." It was not easy, but the hardest "good bye" to say was to his loyal, faithful dog, Jack.

Then all the family got on the train headed for Oregon. After many long days and endless nights, they arrived at their destination—the Willamette Valley in western Oregon. Grandpa bought ninety-two acres of land close to his daughter's place. Grandpa, Uncle Charley, and Daddy built a large two story house for the family. This house looked very similar to the one they had built in Minnesota, and the family enjoyed living in it for many years. Uncle Charley and Daddy managed the farm together.

Grandpa had worked hard all of his life, and now he had time to go fishing at the Willamette River. In the summer, Daddy or Uncle Charley would take him and Grandmother to the coast where they had bought a small piece of property. They put up a tent, and Grandpa and Grandma had a little vacation for a week or so, until either Uncle Charley or Daddy brought them back home. Grandpa or Grandma never learned to drive, but they did know how to have a good time. They especially enjoyed camping by the ocean.

Uncle Charley and Daddy worked in their large fields of grain and also took care of their sheep, cows, chickens, turkeys, and ducks. However, during the hop harvest season, they found time to work in the hop fields. The fields of hops were close to the farm, and the extra cash they received always came in handy. They did whatever needed to be done. They picked hops, ran the equipment, and weighed the hops seeing how many pounds each picker had picked by the end of the day.

One day Uncle Charley and Daddy noticed that a new family by the name of Kendall had come to pick hops. There were three pretty girls and some younger boys in the family. Daddy watched them having fun working happily together. Someone started singing, and soon the family began to harmonize their beautiful voices together as they worked. Uncle Charley and Daddy worked as close to the girls as they could, and listened to the girls eagerly discussing the fact that they were able to save money to go to a boarding school that fall. When Daddy heard the name Laurelwood Academy, he knew they must be Seventh-day Adventists. Now that was electrifying, and it did not take long to strike up a conversation with the girls.

Marjorie, the youngest of the girls, was an adventurer and lots of fun to be around. Uncle Charley and Daddy had recently bought a new Oakland car. It was much more luxurious than the Model Ts they had been driving. When they took the girls for a ride, Marjorie let Daddy know she did not believe that this car belonged to him and Uncle Charley. Since they had been driving the boss' equipment, she felt sure they were just trying to make her think this car belonged to them.

Marjorie turned everything into fun and happiness, and she was a true Christian loving the Lord with all of her sweet heart. Time sped by. The better he knew her the more he liked her. Yes, he might as well admit it. He couldn't help loving this vivacious girl with the happy disposition. The sun smiled tenderly on them. In the evening the moon rose with its creamy light creeping up the sky and the stars melting in it. There was one question that Daddy needed answered. *Would Marjorie be willing to spend the rest of her life with him?*

Chapter 18

Their First Home

Marjorie sent Daddy a card that said:

I lost my heart when I met you,
So I am minus one, you see.
I can't live unless you give
Your own dear heart to me.

Spring with dancing feet and flower-filled arms came flitting over the fields and meadows. Daddy and Mother were married in a simple, outdoor, June wedding in 1930 among the blooming flowers and cherry trees. She was the prettiest bride Daddy had ever seen, and he was the happiest groom, and, well, this was the first wedding he had ever had the privilege of attending in his whole life!!

They moved into a cute, tiny house on the home place and lived there for a little over a year, cozy and cramped for more room. Soon after their dear baby, Bobby, was born, they moved to a farm about two and a half miles from the home where they had been living.

This larger house sat on a hill overlooking the valley below. A big barn, not far from the house, was where they milked the cows and stored the hay for winter. A hand pump used for pumping water for the house was located between the barn and the house. By using a little trough, Daddy could also pump water straight into a large watering tank to water all the cattle. A wooden gate, big enough to drive a truck through, was a part of the barnyard enclosure.

Later, as the years sped by, my brother Bobby and I spent happy times climbing and swinging on this gate. We could see Old Highway 99 in the valley below, and we pretended those speeding cars were our own and imagined where we were going and what we were going to see.

The depression had hit, making money scarce. I was the second child and was born at home. The doctor, quick and confident, and his wife, who was a nurse, came to our house, which was located many miles out in the country, to help bring me into the world. That first night after my daddy tucked me into my little bed and everyone had gone home, Daddy finally blew out the kerosene lamp and headed for bed. I started crying. Daddy found a match and lit the lamp again. I looked around contentedly, and nothing seemed to be wrong. Again Daddy blew out the lamp and headed for bed. I started crying again. *What could be wrong?* Daddy lit the lamp another time. Immediately I quit crying. Daddy smiled and thought, *you little rascal* and blew out the light the third time. He waited a few minutes and after a short time of protesting, I fell asleep.

We had little money, but my parents were busy and happy working together on the small farm. I remember many joyful hours in this older country home. In the springtime we had an abundant variety of wild flowers to gather and bring to Mother until she didn't have another empty vase to fill.

The only miserable times that I can remember were in the winter when it got dark early in the evening, and Mother went to the barn to help Daddy milk the cows. Mother hated to leave us alone, and she learned to milk cows very fast. Daddy impressed upon my brother's mind that he was two years older than I, and he was responsible for taking care of me—a job my brother took very seriously!! I was not happy when Mother shut the door behind her and left us in the house alone. However, my parents never knew how dejected I was or why we were such "good" children and in no way got into any trouble while they were gone until years later. When I became an adult I heard my mother telling a friend why she had such strong hands and could massage for hours. Milking cows is a great exercise for the hands especially when time is a premium because you have two small children waiting in the house. When she mentioned how worried she had been that something would happen to her little children, but it never did because we were so good, I had to tell her a story.

My five-year-old brother, Bobby, didn't want any crying little three-year-old sister to take care of while his parents were busy milking the cows. He came up with an ingenious idea.

We had seen our pet kitty catch a mouse a few days before. If the mouse lay still, the cat lost interest in it, but if it moved, the cat pounced on the mouse. Bobby explained to me that we were like the mouse. We must sit very quietly and not move so whatever or whoever was looking in the windows at us would think we were dead and not try to get us. I remembered sitting frozen with fear listening to the sound of the rain and the wind's strange, wild howl as it made the branches of the trees make a scary, scratching sound against the house. The old kerosene lamp made long flickering shadows on the wall that would not stop moving

I sat petrified staring first at one black window and then the other until my big brother informed me I didn't look "dead." I must keep my eyes closed or at least partly closed. I do not remember how long or how many evenings were spent this way, but Mother said we were always very happy to see her when she came into the house, and she was delighted that we never seemed to get into trouble, get hurt, or mess things up—like turning over the kerosene lamp—when she was gone.

We children had a dog, a cat and a little goat to take care of. We loved these animals and enjoyed watching them play together. Sometimes it was the baby goat chasing the dog and cat. Sometimes it was the dog or even the cat that was doing the chasing, but they always seemed to find something new and interesting to keep our attention like the time the little goat climbed on top of our Model A Ford and was jumping up and down. She soon learned that was "off limits."

We got a separator, a machine with a large bowl at the top that a person poured milk into. The milk went through the machine as someone turned the handle around and around. The cream came out one little spout and the milk came out another little spout separating the cream from the milk. We sold the cream to a creamery that had a big truck that came by and took the ten-gallon cans of cream to their processing plant. We were sent a check from the creamery once a month. This was a large part of our income, and my parents made it stretch as far as possible.

One day Daddy planned to go to Salem on business, and Mother needed to get groceries and some other things. We were out of money. Although we lived only fourteen miles from Salem, we went to town only about once a month. The check from the creamery would be arriving the next day, but Daddy had to go to town that very day.

Mother had always been careful to pay tithe on any income we received. She did have the tithe money from our last check in the house, but of course she would not use it. Finally she decided since a check from the creamery would be coming the next day, she could "borrow" the tithe money. This she did and got the things needed in town.

The next day the check from the creamery did not arrive. This was the only time during our years of selling cream to the creamery that the check did not come on time. It took many weeks for that lost check to finally appear. Mother decided she would never "borrow tithe money" again.

Chapter 19

The Miracle Place at Falls City

The depression ravenously devoured men's jobs and robbed many of our neighbors of their farms. This depression covered the land, and few escaped its iron hand.

Daddy was cutting wood for a few dollars a chord on a nice eighty-acre piece of land, which he felt was an exceptionally fine farm. The ranch we were renting was not expensive, but Daddy wanted us to have a place that belonged to us.

"Would you like to buy some real estate?" a man from the Federal Land Bank asked one day. "We have two good farms that will be repossessed. There is this eighty-acre farm and another one hundred sixty-acre farm that will be for sale soon."

What a break! Daddy was walking on air. Both places were excellent farms, and he could not wait to tell Mother our good fortune.

"Mr. Anderson said we could have either one to rent for three years. At the end of three years, our rent will be used as a down payment. After that, we can make crop payments," he told Mother.

Mother looked at him and did not say a word. *We are getting an opportunity of a lifetime. What could be the matter?* Daddy wondered.

"What about a Christian school?" she asked. "We have been planning to move where the children can go to a Christian school. Remember?"

"No, I had not remembered," Daddy explained, "It had slipped my mind when hearing about the available opportunity. Now I did not say a word. *What would be the right thing to do?*" Finally he replied, "We'll move by a Christian school even if we have to live in a tent!"

The pastor knew of my parent's decision to be by a Christian school where we children would get the best education possible. He told them of an excellent little country school located at Falls City, Oregon. Mother's cousin, Martha Fisher, lived there. My parents wasted no time in going to Falls City. School would soon be starting, and they must find a place to live.

Selling hatching eggs was a good business at that time. We found a wonderful five acre place with two chicken houses big enough for one thousand hens and two brooder houses—just what we wanted. This home had electricity and also running water. No more carrying water from the pump or lighting the kerosene lamp. We all liked the big comfortable home with two extra bedrooms upstairs. Bob and I had our rooms picked out before anyone even asked the price. But the price—that was the problem.

"I am sorry," Daddy told the family. "We can never get this place. The price is too high. It may not be too high for such a nice place, but it is a lot more money than we can afford."

The next Sunday Mother said, "Let's go to Falls City."

"Why? We have looked at everything." Daddy answered.

"Please, let's just go anyway."

All of us had been praying the Lord would help us find the place He wanted us to have. We drove to Falls City and went to visit Cousin Martha. When she saw us coming up the driveway, she came out all smiles.

"You got my letter already?" she beamed. These were the days before many rural families in our area had telephones. We certainly did not have one.

"No, we didn't get any letter."

"I sent you a letter telling you that Mr. Schrader just dropped the price on his place. He will lose one or both of his places if he doesn't sell right away. You can buy the place for half the price he was asking last week."

Cousin Martha and her husband had sold a ranch in Minnesota before coming to Oregon. They had money they wanted to invest and suggested they loan us the full amount of money needed to pay for our dream place.

Early the next morning Daddy headed for Oregon City, where Mr. Schrader lived. *Let's see, Main Street should not be hard to find.* Main Street went one way to the river and the other way back up the hill. Daddy looked at every house on the street, but could not find the number for the home. No one seemed to know where the Schraders lived.

Time was being lost, and Daddy continually prayed that he would be able to find the place. After hours of searching, a man told him that when the road was surveyed, the surveying crew went right over the hill. "There is a short road on the other side of that hill," he said, "and I believe it is Main Street."

"How do I get there?"

High School was already letting out for the day. Daddy still had not found the place, and no one knew where the Schrader's lived. Then he met three boys hiking up the hill.

"Could you tell me where Mr. Schrader lives?" Daddy asked.

"Never heard of him," they answered.

"I hear they have a real pretty girl," he told them.

The boys looked at each other. "That must be Maryanne, one said. "Yes, see that white house back there? I think that is the family you want to see."

At the end of the road Daddy saw two houses. On one he saw the number he had been searching for all day. What a relief. Then disappointment hit when he saw that no one was at home. *What should he do?* Daddy sat in his car awhile pondering the situation and wondering what to do next. After a little while the neighbor came over. "Are you looking for the Schraders? They are gone and won't be home tonight. Mrs. Schrader and Maryanne are picking hops and are camped at the hop yard. Mr. Schrader goes there after work and doesn't come home."

"Where does he work?"

Daddy called his workplace and asked if Mr. Schrader could come to the phone.

"No," was the answer. "He is running heavy equipment and cannot leave it."

"Please have him call me when he gets off work."

Daddy waited in his car, and then went back into the house when the neighbor called him.

"Mr. Schrader, I am here to buy your place."

"I will stop by and get my wife and daughter, and we will be right home," he assured Daddy.

Again Daddy sat waiting in his car. Mr. Schrader came and walked slowly over to talk with my daddy. He had a letter in his hand. "I stopped at the mailbox just now and got this letter," he said, opening a letter from Falls City. "In this letter they told me not to sell the place. They are very anxious to get the place, and since they have the mortgage, and want it back, you can see I cannot sell this place to you. I am sorry to have caused you all this bother."

"Mr. Schrader," Daddy said, pulling a letter out of his pocket. "Did you write this letter?"

"Yes."

"Is this your signature?"

"Yes."

"In this letter you said the place is for sale, and I have come to buy the place."

Mr. Schrader stood for a moment, thinking.

"And I will sell it," he answered. "When I am through with something, I drop it like a hot potato."

He signed a statement for the city of Falls City telling them that Otto Mitchell was taking over the place, and then handed the statement to Daddy. My daddy drove the sixty miles home that evening a happy man.

The next day he went back to Falls City to the City Recorder's Office and showed them the statement from Mr. Schrader. He handed the man in charge the money to cover the mortgage. The man said, "Well, it looks like you got it." Then he signed all the papers.

We knew God had worked a miracle for us to get this

nice place where Bobby and I would have the privilege of a Christian education.

We did not know until nearly twenty years later when Daddy and Mother were looking over some old papers that on the bottom of Mr. Schrader's mortgage contract was written, "This place cannot be sold without the permission of the city of Falls City."

Chapter 20

Moving

We loaded our truck with furniture and our other belongings that could be packed into it. Our excitement ran high, for we were moving to Falls City, Oregon, a beautiful little place twenty-five miles west of Salem.

When Daddy backed the truck up to the house to start unloading, he noticed that the people who were supposed to be moved out were still living in the house, and it appeared that they were not planning to move very soon.

The man came out and said, "You have to give me thirty days written notice."

"Mr. Miller*," Daddy said, "You knew we were coming over today, and you knew this over thirty days ago. Get a truck, and I will help you move **right now**. Do you have a

* Names have been changed

place where we can move your things?"

He hesitated. "We-l-l yes," he answered.

It took two truckloads to get him completely moved from the place, and then we moved in.

Mr. Miller told my Grandpa Kendall, "There is a man (talking about Daddy) I can **never** like."

However, in a week Mr. Miller came to visit us. "Could I rent that building from you for a couple weeks?"

We had plenty of room so Daddy told him, "Sure. You just go ahead and use it."

Mr. Miller made puffed corn and puffed wheat. He put the grain in a machine, built up the pressure, and with one mighty bang the corn or wheat would blast out of the machine clear across the building down a chute he had made for the process. Mr. Miller and my daddy became good friends. We had all the puffed corn and wheat we could eat while he used the building for nearly two years rent free.

Bob would be starting to the school located only one mile away the next Monday. Mother had bought him new clothes, and I felt left out. In fact I was very jealous. However, Mother promised that when I went to school, there would probably be some new clothes for me then, too.

When Daddy saw the teacher, he could hardly believe his eyes. The first time he had seen Peggy, the teacher, she was a little girl ten years old.

Peggy said, "Oh, Otto, I remember the first time I ever saw you. I was embarrassed and climbed an apple tree and threw apples at you."

Daddy had not been very old himself. Peggy could drive the horses at a young age. She could plow or do whatever needed to be done just like a hired man. Whatever she did she put her whole heart into it. Daddy knew it would be a good school year. She was a little lady, and some of the eighth grade boys looked twice her size, but there was no question about who was in control. The pastor had been right, and my brother has always maintained that Peggy was the best teacher he ever had.

We were happy living in our comfortable home snuggled between the mountains, under the trees, and surrounded by flowers. Would we really not be able to pay our bills and make a living on this place? Would we really have the problems here that some neighbors predicted?

Chapter 21

Challenges

Our neighbors told us we could not raise chickens. Nobody could raise chickens in the Falls City area. We may have bought a nice layout, and these buildings *had* been used to raise chickens, but didn't we know that no one had raised chickens here for the last few years. It could not be done.

What did they mean? We had bought a chicken ranch. Of course my parents planned to raise chickens. "Your chickens will be stolen. Don't waste your money trying to raise chickens. It can't be done, so people have stopped trying. The chickens are always stolen," we were told.

One night after coming home from a school board meeting, Daddy went to check the chicken house. The back door to the building stood open. That seemed strange. We never left it open. The next morning we counted the chickens. It is not an easy job to count hundreds of chickens. The best we could figure, we were missing ten to twenty.

We got a big collie dog named Cuffy. He was a good watchdog—when he was awake. The problem seemed to be he liked to sleep. At night after everyone had gone to bed, Daddy would sneak out of the house with a treat for Cuffy. He then started watching for Daddy. Whenever Cuffy heard a footstep, he was wide awake looking for a handout.

One night Daddy heard a car come down the road making a lot of noise. It stopped, and he could hear people working on the car. This happened the second night. On the third night when this happened, Cuffy began barking, and Daddy knew someone had come to get the chickens.

Uncle Charley and Daddy had worked as detectives for several years, so this was something he knew how to take care of. Daddy had gotten nearly to the chicken house when his feet made some noise on the gravel. He heard the fellows start to run for the road. These guys were going pretty fast, but to speed them up a bit, Daddy put a couple bullets in the ground not far from them.

Daddy had a pretty good idea who the two men were when he went to the sheriff's office the next morning. By the looks on their faces, he was pretty sure they also knew who he was. Daddy explained what happened and told the sheriff his background and what he planned to do to take care of the chicken-stealing problem. After that, we never had any trouble with someone trying to steal our chickens. Other people started raising a few chickens in the Falls City area and we never heard of anyone having any chicken-stealing troubles. It was a great place to live.

A large field across the road from our place lay vacant because no one was farming it. Daddy asked the neighbor who owned it if he could rent the land. My folks wanted to raise some wheat.

"You can't raise any wheat on that land," the neighbor informed my daddy. "That land has been cursed. No one tries to farm it anymore."

Daddy told the neighbor he still wanted to rent the land. After Daddy continually requested the chance to farm the land and see what it would do, the neighbor reluctantly agreed. Other neighbors were concerned as they noticed the hours of work we put into preparing and planting the field. Daddy informed each and every person that he was not concerned about the curse. Of course we continually prayed that God would reward our efforts.

The wheat grew, and when autumn arrived, we harvested a bumper crop grown on that cursed field. It was important for people to know that our God was stronger than any curse anyone could put on the land. God had been faithful, and we praised His name.

It takes time to get started in a new business, and the bills kept coming in. Mother and we children knew how to take care of the chickens, so, if Daddy could find work that would pay us cash, we could pay the bills and get some needed items. Many people were out of work. *Would he be able to find something?*

Chapter 22

Getting and Giving Help

Green grass covered the meadow, and the creek sang merrily as it ran down the hillside carpeted with wild flowers. The weather stayed comfortable and fairly warm for early springtime in western Oregon.

My daddy always enjoyed working out in God's creation, and he was making some much needed cash peeling poles for a neighbor. My grandparents lived across the road from where Daddy was working. Grandpa Kendall had told Daddy about the job, and they worked together. The pay promised was excellent, and the poles they were peeling were giving up their bark without a fuss. Grandpa Kendall and Daddy were thankful for this job where they had worked several weeks.

A caterpillar pulled the poles out of the woods, and a loader put them onto a truck after they were peeled. The truck took the peeled logs to the railroad freight yard where they were loaded onto the flatbeds of the train and then taken to

Seattle, Washington.

"I think I will quit this job," Daddy told Grandpa. "There seems to be something wrong. I just have a really bad feeling about it."

"If you quit, I will quit too," Grandpa answered.

Daddy had made it a habit not to work in a situation where he felt dishonesty was being practiced. This job located so close to our place could have been ideal, but still Daddy recognized the time for him to quit had come.

Grandpa told the owners, Mr. Palmerton* and his sons, that they had quit the job and asked for the check that would pay for the work already done. The check he received turned out to be about half the amount Grandpa thought they should have gotten.

"What shall we do?" he asked Daddy. They were being paid by the foot, which means they were being paid a certain amount for each foot of the pole where they had cleaned off the bark. Daddy had measured the poles that were peeled and kept track of all the work done. Now the owner insisted that he had given them all the money they would get.

"We'll go to the Labor Commission," Daddy told my grandpa. The Labor Commission is a part of the government that helps people who are not treated fairly by the person they are working for. "We will not accept this." Daddy told Mr. Palmerton. He became upset. "Forget it," he shouted. "That is all I owe you, and that is all you will get."

Our family started praying about the problem. Grandpa and Daddy had worked hard, and now it looked like they would never get the money they had rightfully earned. Grandpa and Daddy drove to Salem, Oregon, twenty-five miles away, and went to the Capitol Building. There they found the Labor Commission Office and spoke to the man

---

* Names have been changed

at the desk. He pressed a little button, and a young lawyer came in.

"Please take over this case," he told the young lawyer.

After hearing the problem and taking a few notes, the lawyer turned to Grandpa and Daddy and said, "I want you to meet me tomorrow at eight o'clock in the morning at the railroad freight yard."

That afternoon the lawyer contacted the company buying the peeled poles and found out how many feet of poles had been shipped to them. Since Grandpa and my daddy were the only ones on the job peeling the poles, he knew how much they had peeled.

"Where is the man we have come to see?" the lawyer asked, when they arrived at the freight yard the next morning.

"He is the man up there loading that car," Daddy answered.

"Mr. Palmerton, we want to talk with you," the lawyer said.

"I'll come down when I get this loaded," he shouted.

"You come down right now, or you will be in court tomorrow," the lawyer answered.

Daddy could tell that Mr. Palmerton felt very angry. Everyone could tell he was angry by the way he came, but he did climb down off the pile of poles he had been loading onto the train car. His face showed the ugly snarls of thoughts filtering through his head. The lawyer showed Mr. Palmerton the figures. "You have the check for these men in three days," he commanded Mr. Palmerton.

They got the check in three days, but the Palmertons were pretty upset with Daddy and Grandpa. They had only gotten paid what they had been promised, but obviously the Palmertons had not planned to give them their fair share.

While at my grandparent's place, a week later, Daddy noticed the Palmertons were having trouble starting their caterpillar. First one person would crank and then another. Daddy decided they needed a little help.

"You had better not go over there," Grandpa told him. "They are pretty mad."

"I think I can handle that," Daddy answered, and went to see what he could do. They looked at Daddy surprised when he walked up and said, "I noticed you are having a little trouble. Maybe I can help." Daddy did a little adjusting here and there on the motor and soon had the equipment going. They did not say a word, and neither did Daddy.

Some time later as Mother and Daddy were driving out to my grandparent's place again, Daddy noticed a car stuck beside the road. He stopped to help. It was one of the Palmerton boys. It took quite a bit of hard work to get the car out on the road again so the Palmerton kid could go on his way. This time he smiled and said, "Thank you."

Daddy was determined to have no hard feelings against the Palmertons. They needed to pay what they had agreed to pay in the first place, and it had taken quite a bit of Daddy's time for the favor he gave them—showing the importance of keeping their word.

Chapter 23

God Knew the Future

We enjoyed living on our small five-acre parcel where we had a miniature barn for our one cow with plenty of pasture. We also raised a big garden, a couple acres of strawberries, and a thousand healthy red hens laying big, brown eggs. The eggs had to be gathered three times a day to keep them from getting cracked. The company buying the eggs, to be used for hatching baby chickens, paid us well for these eggs that we shipped to California.

When the doctor said we needed to move to a drier climate because of my brother's health, my parents lost no time in trying to find a place where he would soon be well again. At that time the man who bought our eggs came to see us from California. He had arranged for another company to buy eggs from us for awhile, and then he would start buying again in a few months, he told us.

Daddy told him we were planning to move. "Don't sell the chickens," he said. "Move them with you. Selling hatching eggs is a booming business. You will make a lot of money by staying in it."

Mother had been praying that when it was time to sell the chickens and get out of the business of selling hatching eggs, the company buying from us would stop buying the eggs. She told Daddy, "Now is the time to sell."

"The business looks good," he answered. "It isn't like we don't have a company to buy the eggs."

Mother felt that she had asked God for a sign to know when to sell, and she wanted to sell. We sold. We did not look for another chicken ranch when we moved to central Oregon. Instead we bought a forty acre farm.

In less than a year, many people who were in the chicken business lost everything they had. The company we had been selling to went bankrupt. That made us feel sad, but we praised God for giving us the privilege of being in partnership with Him Who has divine foreknowledge and was leading us in a way that saved us from great financial loss.

Chapter 24

Johnny

The United Sates was in a war called World War II from 1941 to 1945. This brought many shortages to our community including rationing on gas and some items like sugar and coffee. Many things were hard to find. It was hard to get tires for the car, but the biggest shortage for my parents happened to be where to get farm machinery.

We had bought a small forty acre farm in central Oregon and needed machinery to run it. It appeared that no one wanted to sell their used machinery until they could get something better, and new machinery seemed almost non-existent.

Our order had been on the list for a new John Deere Model H tractor for months. The crops needed to be planted, and we still had nothing to work with. Grandpa Kendall brought a nervous little brown horse for Daddy to use. A neighbor said he could borrow his big white horse for awhile. Now we had a team. Daddy was ready to start the spring work.

"That horse is a runaway," the neighbor said as Daddy took the large animal from the corral. Daddy had grown up using horses on the farm. "This horse would have been no problem for me," he said, "if I had not hit a rock which broke the tongue of the corrugator."

Daddy's leg caught between the whiffletree and the even-er, making it impossible to remove his foot and threw him on the ground. When the big white horse looked around and saw Daddy on the ground, he lunged forward, and the team took off dragging him by one leg. Daddy threw the free leg over the one that was caught so as not to be pulled apart. The reins were in his hands, but he could not get them pulled up to where he could control the horses. Just before the runaway team hit the fence, Daddy pulled enough on one line to turn the horses. This put the brown horse ahead, and he pulled his leg from the trap where it had gotten caught. Being quick on his feet, Daddy jumped up and grabbed the horses' bits. Now he could control those runaway horses.

God had protected Daddy in a marvelous way by not letting the horses drag him over any rocks or through the fence. He hobbled to the barn where he let the horses out to pasture as he continually watched that big white horse. The moment that cantankerous animal got his freedom; he turned and kicked at Daddy with both hind feet. He ran across the pasture and then jumped the cattle guard in one powerful leap and headed for another neighbor's garden. With the neighbor's help, they captured the horse, and took him back home.

We continued to pray for a tractor. How could we get the crops in and taken care of that summer? One neighbor said,

"You will never get a new tractor. Very few new tractors are being shipped in."

"We are only second on the list for a new one," Mother told him.

"That doesn't mean a thing," he answered. "I happen to know. If someone comes in with six bottles of whisky and offers it as a gift, even if the tractor *should* go to you, you will not get it."

Mother looked at him and said, "We need a tractor badly, and we have been praying about it. My God is bigger than six bottles of whiskey."

A few days before a tractor was to arrive, the man on the list before us came into the store to see when he could get his tractor. He happened to be bragging about the good used tractor he had just gotten.

"Then you don't need this new one," answered the owner.

"Oh, sure I do," he replied. "I have a friend who I will sell it to."

"The government will not allow us to do that. If you have equipment to run your farm, the next person on the list will receive the tractor," the owner told him.

We thanked God for His blessings as Daddy drove our truck to town to get the tractor that had been ordered many months before.

Bob, looked at that tractor and asked, "Dad, can I drive it home?"

"Why should you? We have the truck here to haul it." Then Daddy looked at Bob's face, and said, "If you want to drive it home, we will follow you."

Daddy and I, coming behind in the truck, watched my proud, teen-age brother drive that new John Deere Model H tractor home. He had a wonderful summer working it on the farm. We all considered it our miracle tractor.

I didn't think it was fair that Bob got to drive the new tractor all the time. In fact, Bob and I had gotten into a pretty heavy discussion over the matter. Even though Bob insisted that I was not capable of handling Johnny H, Daddy decided it was time to let me have a chance. I knew I could do it, and felt it would be a lot more fun than working in the garden or helping in the house all the time.

After a terrific struggle fighting with Johnny H trying to keep him where he should be going down two rows of potatoes and taking out several feet of the little green potato plants, I decided that the tractor had a mind of its own and never again felt jealous of Bob being able to run the new tractor up and down those long rows of potatoes.

Chapter 25

Our New Tractor

When we had moved to this farm five years before, our neighbors told us the ground was not any good, and we would have a hard time making a living on it. Maybe that is the reason we got it for such a reasonable price. Our family felt it was an answer to prayer.

Daddy hauled in many truckloads of fertilizer from a sheep farm about fifteen miles away. He spread this over the fields and also grew cover crops to build up the land. Our place produced well. We worked long, hard hours, and the corn, potatoes and alfalfa responded beautifully. Daddy felt he needed more land to farm. Daddy and Bob had kept the one small tractor busy, and we needed another larger tractor in order to keep up with the work. Our John Deere H tractor was too small to plow the thick sod of the land we wanted to rent.

Tractors were still hard to get. We had had an order in for a new one for nearly a year. *What were we going to do?* This was a high priority on our prayer list. *What should we do about a tractor?* Both Bob and I were away at Columbia Academy, a boarding school, during the school year, and the bills from the school were high.

Les, our neighbor, had decided he wanted a larger tractor. He owned the same kind of tractor we had on order.

"I am going to sell my tractor," he told Daddy one day. "Would you be interested in buying it? I will be asking the same price for it as a new one would cost."

Daddy looked at his tractor. One tire would have to be replaced, and he knew it had had hard use, but we had to have a tractor if we rented that other forty acres to the west. Daddy talked it over with Mother. It seemed like the answer to our prayers.

"I will take your tractor," Daddy told Les.

"You don't need to be in a hurry," he answered. "It will be here for you."

What a blessing! God had answered our prayers for the needed equipment to run the farm. Now we could get the land joining our place before someone else rented it.

A few days later, Mother and Daddy got into the car with their checkbook. They were excited about getting the very much needed tractor. Daddy drove up the neighbor's driveway just as he and his wife, with another couple, were getting ready to leave for the movies on this Saturday night.

"I have come to pay for the tractor," Daddy told Les.

"I sold it yesterday," he answered.

Daddy said little as he got back into the car to go home. He said **quite** a little to Mother on the way home. *What a* *great neighborly thing to do! His word was nothing!! He had promised! Now what were we going to do?* We had rented more land on the promise of another tractor, and now we had no equipment big enough to run it.

Mother reminded Daddy of the many ways the Lord had led in the past. "God may have something better in store," she told him. Daddy said later, "I had no idea what that would be and had a hard time getting into the sweet, trusting mood Marjorie was experiencing."

Monday morning Daddy saw a pickup drive down our driveway. It was a cold, windy day, and he invited the man to come inside the warm house by the fire. "You will be getting a new tractor," he told Daddy. "We expect the shipment tomorrow."

On the way to town the next day in our truck, the train went by. Daddy saw two tractors chained down on one of the flat bed train cars. By the time he arrived at the warehouse, the two tractors were being unloaded.

"Take your pick," the owner told him.

Daddy said, "I thought of what my feelings would be if I had bought that older piece of equipment just two days before the new one arrived. This time Marjorie and I both thanked God for not letting us make the mistake of buying the older tractor with the ruined tire."

Mother repeated her favorite quotation, "We have nothing to fear for the future, only as we forget the way the Lord has led us thus far."

In a few short months we would have the privilege of seeing God's hand working in a very direct manner in ways we could never even imagine.

Chapter 26

The Big Load of Potatoes

Daddy was trucking potatoes over the mountains from central Oregon to the Willamette Valley selling them to the stores. He tried to get orders ahead and then pile our truck full of potatoes and deliver them to the customers.

One day on the way home, Daddy stopped at a big store to see if he could bring them some potatoes.

"Yes," answered the manager. "I would take a whole six-ton truckload. I need them early Sunday morning."

Daddy loaded our new truck with one hundred-pound sacks of potatoes. Mother and he left before daylight Sunday morning and arrived at the store early.

When Daddy backed the truck up to the store, he noticed three men sitting on a bench located close to the door that he went through back and forth carrying the heavy sacks of potatoes. They were dressed in medium dressy outfits, and they did not offer to help, but talked together in tones too low for Daddy to hear what they were saying.

Daddy unloaded one hundred and twenty sacks of potatoes all by himself. The men were not doing anything but watching him and talking together. When he finished unloading the truck, he went to get paid for the potatoes.

The manager went to the cash register and handed Daddy over $500.00 in cash. No one had ever done this before. He had always gotten money by check if it was a large amount. This was a long time ago, and it was a very large amount of money to us. Daddy put the money in his wallet and got into the truck.

The three men who had been loitering around doing nothing walked to their older-looking, light-colored Chevrolet.

"Don't let them know," Daddy told Mother, "but keep watch and see if they are following."

"Yes, I can see them coming."

"Then we can't head for home over the mountains."

Daddy turned towards the main part of town up one street and down the other. *Where was a policeman?* The car stayed behind. *How could he lose those three men driving a car and him driving the big truck?* If it had not been Sunday, he would have deposited the money into a bank. By this time he had run around town and was heading back through town towards home. *What was he going to do?* He had to ditch those three men some way, but they were right behind him.

Early that morning on the way to town, Daddy noticed a construction crew building a new house. A large pile of lumber had been stacked by the side of it.

Now Daddy approached some railroad tracks where the railway cars were being switched. The lights were flashing, and they stopped to wait. His thoughts were whirling. *Something had to be done!* Daddy waited while the slow-moving train came ready to cross the road, then he raced the truck's motor and shot across the track in front of the train. The men in the car behind had no time to get across the track before the long train blocked the way. Daddy drove as fast as he could to the place where he remembered the pile of lumber and pulled the truck in behind. Soon Daddy and Mother saw the car that had been following them speeding up the highway. They waited. In about twenty minutes or so, the car went rushing back to town. Daddy started the truck, pulled out from behind that lumber pile, and kept it wide open almost all the way home!

What a God we have. We do not believe that train "just happened" to block the road at that particular time. We believe it was God's way of answering their prayers and giving Daddy the thought to drive right in front of that moving train.

Chapter 27

God's Police Car

Summer was passing us by, and fall came close behind. It had been a good season. Making one's living on the farm meant that the summer and fall months must supply whatever income we needed to live on the rest of the year.

The seven acres of corn we had planted in the spring, and then hoed, cultivated, and watered all summer had responded to our hours and hours of hard work. Beautiful, big ears of juicy sweet corn waited to be picked and sold to the stores.

This was a particularly busy time. We not only picked, and sorted, but also looked at each ear of corn to see that it was well matured but not over-ripe. We checked to see that not a single worm was hiding someplace before filling the big gunny sacks that held ten dozen ears of corn.

Our attention to details had paid well, for the stores eagerly looked forward to getting their fresh roasting ears from us. They knew they would be getting the best, and my parents tried never to sell anything but the best.

We all enjoyed selling our vegetables to the Indians. We had sold to them before we started selling to the stores. They knew us well and trusted us. These people were our friends and knew what good corn and other vegetables looked like. They would buy a full sack of corn at a time to eat and dry for winter.

The days were pleasant at the Indian Reservation. The people at almost every house where we stopped bought something. It might be apples from our orchard, or squash, and other vegetables from the garden. They appreciated this fresh food, and appeared to know that some of the very old people who could not afford to buy anything would receive something from us—a few apples, an onion or two, and some corn—whatever we had on hand.

My parents also bought boxes of the little books *Steps to Christ* written by Ellen White and gave them to their customers and other friends. After listening to people telling them how much they enjoyed the book and how it had changed their lives, I decided that I would read the book and find out what was so wonderful about it. One summer afternoon I took the book and found a nice cool place under a Juniper tree and started reading. Although I was only eleven or twelve at the time, I read that book over and over. At an early age I learned that I was very important to God. No matter what happened or what I did He would always love me.

My parents were great teachers. We went to church almost every week and had family devotions nearly every day. I knew sin was dreadful because it hurt the heart of God, but for some reason I never put it all together until I read the book *Steps to Christ*. I don't remember ever talking about my decisions with anyone. I just made up my mind I was going to obey my God because I could always trust Him. If I used His Word, the Bible, as my operating instructions, it would keep me from making a lot of mistakes.

However, I had a problem. Knowing myself the way I did

I knew I would never be good enough to go to heaven. It was too beautiful, too special, and too perfect. I missed the whole idea God was trying to tell me. One evening kneeling beside my bed with tears streaming down my cheeks, I explained my problem to God. During the night I had a beautiful dream that I shall never forget. I was traveling up a slippery path and kept sliding and was ready to fall, but when I looked up to Jesus (I didn't see Him, but knew He was there) I was perfectly safe. I learned not to worry about being "good enough" which of course I could not be, but what I needed to do was keep my eyes on Jesus and follow Him. I knew the greatest thing in life was to never sever my relationship with my Lord. It was the best relationship a person could ever have. He would take the responsibility of getting me to heaven. Not only was this a comforting feeling, it was exciting, wonderful, and something I didn't want to lose.

This became a part of my life, so a few years later when "the cutest guy in college" asked me to marry him, my first thought was for us to ask God together what His will would be. Delmer and I prayed together. My best girl friend had been telling me this guy would never be the right person for me to marry unless I could change!! Although I loved Delmer, I was confused, but during the prayer, the thought struck me that I must not say "no" to this fantastic guy—one of the best decisions of my life. If you would like to hear of some of the exciting adventures God had waiting for us during the next fifty years, read the books *Patti and the Briefcase*, *Patti's Journey in Faith*, and *I Will Lift Up My Eyes*.

Now, back to the time when my parents were selling large sacks of roasting ears picked fresh from their own fields of ripening corn. On this eventful day they had gone to the Indian fishing grounds at Celilo Falls, which was located by the Columbia River many miles away from our home. Celilo

Falls was a very important part of the Native American culture at that time. The people caught most of their yearly supply of salmon there. The falls were beautiful and attracted many tourists during the summer months. Later, when The Dalles Dam was built in 1957, the water covered Celilo Falls and this fishing ground ceased to exist.

The fishing had been good this day, the people were happy, and my parents had sold most of the corn—all twenty-nine sacks. They had only one sack of corn left to sell.

"There is a little store," Daddy said to Mother. "Maybe we can sell the last sack of corn there."

Daddy parked the truck in front of the store and walked inside. Mother waited in the truck. The pay for a whole load of corn, which was a substantial part of the summer's work, filled Daddy's wallet.

Store? This looked more like a saloon and a gambling joint to Daddy. This was not where he wanted to be, but before he could turn and leave, two big men grabbed him by the arms and announced, "Here is a fellow who will gamble with us."

"I don't gamble!" Daddy answered, looking around to see if he could find a friend or someone who knew him, but all were strangers.

"Sure you do."

"I don't know how to gamble."

"We'll teach you."

All this time they were dragging Daddy to the back of the room and were heading to another dark room at the back of the building. The situation did not look good. Daddy felt his only help would be from God, and he asked his Lord and Savior to completely take over and protect him. Would he lose all of his money? What about his life?

Daddy continued to pray as the men commanded him to

put all of his money out on the table. Suddenly while Daddy was praying, the men dropped their hold on him! They rushed out the back door! About a dozen or so other men who had been standing close by, fled out the back door right behind them!!

As Daddy whirled around and dashed to the front of the building, he saw an Oregon State Police car pulling up to the entrance. By the time Daddy got outside, that dark blue car was gone. Mother, who had been sitting right there in the truck, looked at Daddy in surprise when he asked her where the police car had gone. She had not seen it. Just one dead end road went by the saloon, and it ran between the river and a rock wall. There was no place for that car to have gone, but it was not there.

Daddy started the truck and hurried down the road. *Where had that police car gone?* It had disappeared.

"For He shall give his angels charge over thee, to keep thee in all thy ways. Ps 91: 11" Mother repeated when Daddy finished telling her what had happened.

Thank You, Daddy

(For Daddy's 94th Birthday)

I want to thank you, Daddy,
for the example you have been.
You taught us how to look to God
and not to worldly men.
I thank God for your patience
and courage through the years.
You never were too busy
to hear my joys or fears.
Your self-denial for us,
your honesty always
gave us the strength to follow—
"It is honesty that pays."
God says to lead by precept,
and the example you have given—
I want to thank you, Daddy,
for leading us toward heaven.

By Evelyn Wagner

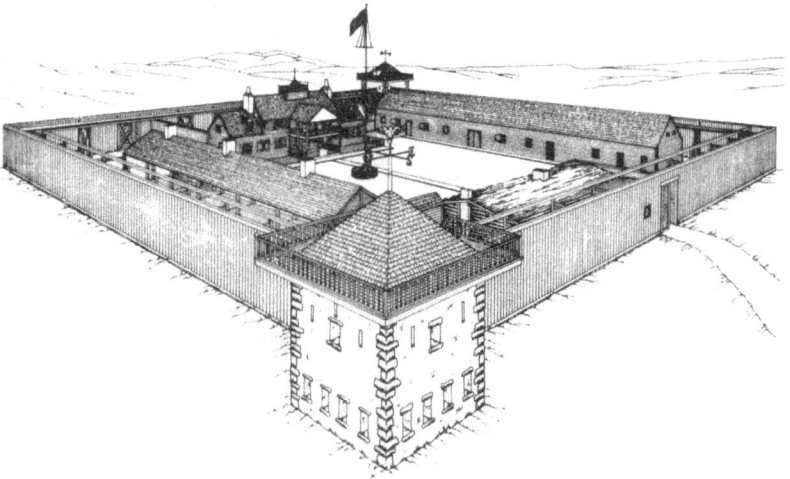

Fort like the one Charley Mitchell, my grandpa,
helped build around 1877 and 1878

Grandpa, Charley Mitchell
About 1890

Grandma, Anna Komm Mitchell,
About 1890

Logs coming into Height O'Land Lake
when Daddy was a boy

The Mitchell's log house at Height O'Land Lake
Left to right: Uncle Charley, Grandpa, Daddy on Grandpa's
Lap, Aunt Anna, Grandma, and Aunt Clara

The Charley Mitchell Family in 1900
Uncle Charley, Grandpa, Daddy, Aunt Anna,
Grandma, and Aunt Clara

This picture of the Mitchell Family was taken around 1906. From left to right: Uncle Charley, Grandpa, Grandma, and Aunt Anna are standing in the back. Daddy is standing in front of Grandpa next to Aunt Clara.

*The house that Grandpa built around 1908 located
three miles north of Detroit Lakes, Minnesota
Left to Right: Uncle Charley, Grandma, Daddy,
Grandpa, Aunt Anna, Aunt Clara, and
Great-Grandpa and Grandma Komm*

Getting the team of horses ready to go someplace

Same house that Grandpa built in 1908 getting a new foundation and a new look in 1980

Detroit Lakes, Minnesota, was called Detroit, Minnesota, when this picture was taken. 1914

This picture was sent on a card to Daddy in Minnesota before his family moved to Oregon saying...

Jefferson, Oregon
January 14, 1918

To Otto Mitchell,

I am going to send you a picture of our house which brother Ole took a short time ago, but it is a very poor picture because it was taken from the wrong side and the grass is so tall in front of the house it doesn't look right, but I suppose that grass looks good to you at this time of the year. We are having a nice mild winter. We don't have any frost and things are growing good...

From your brother in rainy Oregon.
Chris J. Jorgenson

Clara Mitchell
First Day in Oregon, 1919

Charley and Otto Mitchell
First Day in Oregon, 1919

Marjorie (Kendall) Mitchell, 1928

Otto Mitchell, 1929

Grandpa holding six-week-old Bobby Mitchell with Wesley
and Jim Jorgenson, Anna's boys, standing behind in 1931

Daddy out working the back field with
Fordson Tractor, about 1932

Otto and Marjorie Mitchell and the Oakland car

Anna and Charles Mitchell in 1931

Evelyn and Bobby Mitchell, 1937

Marjorie and Otto Mitchell at their 50th
Wedding Anniversary, 1980

Evelyn Wagner and Bob Mitchell at their parents Otto and Marjorie Mitchell's 65th Wedding Anniversary, 1995

INVISIBLE LEADERSHIP STORIES

By Evelyn Wagner

STORIES MY DADDY TOLD ME begins the series with Evelyn's great-great-grandfather, a Scottish soldier, being shipped to America from Scotland to join the British in the American Revolution. Instead, he and his companions joined George Washington and fought to help free the new country from the British rule. Evelyn's great-grandfather sailed around the world many times placing American Ambassadors in other countries. Follow God's leading in the life of her grandfather as he joined a wagon train to go west, became a friend of the great leader Chief Sitting Bull, and later learned to know the God Who had been leading all his life. Watch as God saved her father and family from thieves, financial failure, and potential robbers.

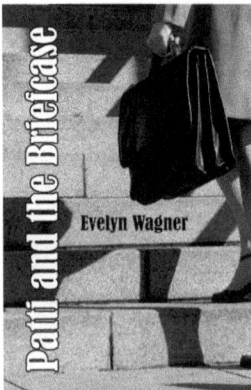

PATTI AND THE BRIEFCASE tells stories of a very shy bride going to Canada with her new husband to sell books. Stories too frightening and embarrassing for Evelyn to tell using her real name, she uses the name "Patti," the pet name her father called her when she was just a little girl.

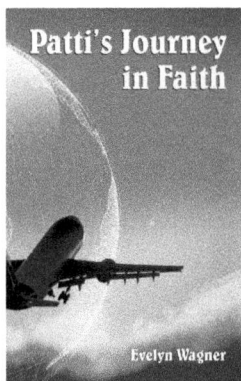

PATTI'S JOURNEY IN FAITH begins at Walla Walla College (University now) with a young couple named Delmer and Evelyn, but known as Del and Patti, in this setting. Travel with them in their struggle to serve their Lord in the challenges of going to college and then starting a new business. This story reveals a life of love, courage, disappointment, laughter, and discovery with the overarching theme of the gracious nearness of God.

FORWARD was the only way to go when Delmer and Evelyn stepped out in faith to start Christian television stations. God opened doors while the enemy built walls that seemed to shut down all progress. Watch God perform miracles when His people are willing to step FORWARD in faith.

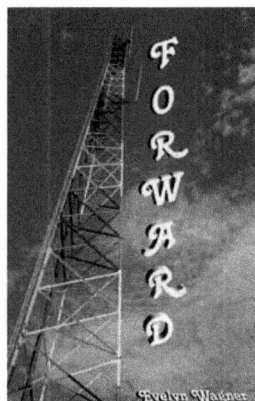

We invite you to view the complete
selection of titles we publish at:

www.TEACHServices.com

Scan with your mobile
device to go directly
to our website.

Please write or email us your praises, reactions, or
thoughts about this or any other book we publish at:

TEACH Services, Inc.
P U B L I S H I N G
www.TEACHServices.com

P.O. Box 954
Ringgold, GA 30736

info@TEACHServices.com

TEACH Services, Inc., titles may be purchased in bulk for
educational, business, fund-raising, or sales promotional use.
For information, please e-mail:

BulkSales@TEACHServices.com

Finally, if you are interested in seeing
your own book in print, please contact us at

publishing@TEACHServices.com

We would be happy to review your manuscript for free.

www.ingramcontent.com/pod-product-compliance
Lightning Source LLC
Chambersburg PA
CBHW060543100426
42742CB00013B/2429

* 9 7 8 1 5 7 2 5 8 5 6 7 6 *